be.
love.

Praise for be. love.

"Christin's new book is the perfect follow-up to *Her Phoenix Rising* because it gets into the HOW. How do I *be. love.?* I also love how Christin breaks down the cornerstones of trauma and how they affect us in so many ways."

— Cheryl Outlaw, Health and Wellness Industry

"*be. love.* is a practical guide infused with authenticity and actionable insights. Each chapter serves as a step on the path to a healthier, happier life."

— Scott Kashman, MHA, FACHE,
President/CEO, Healthcare Executive

"*be. love.* is like a guidebook for anyone who has yearned to take a deeper journey into understanding themselves and their truth but is overwhelmed about where and how to start."

— Tracy Zboril, MSW, co-founder of Soul Happy
and co-pioneer of the Root Cause Healing Movement

"*be. love.* is profound. It presents love as a navigational GPS in a relatable and innovative way. It perfectly captures the right 'next words' after *Her Phoenix Rising.* This book is a gift to the world!"

— Sarah Owen, Business Executive

"Written from the heart of Christin Collins, *be. love.* will captivate you with its profound insights, timely message, and intuitive approach to understanding one of life's most fundamental emotions. It's a simple masterpiece that stands out for its freshness, relevance, intuitiveness, and timeliness."

— Robin Mixon, Chief Financial Officer

be.
love.

Christin Collins

Wellness Writers Press

WELLNESS WRITERS PRESS
An imprint of Pure Ink Press

Paperback ISBN: 979-8-9894541-4-3
Epub ISBN: 979-8-9894541-5-0

wellnesswriterspress.com
www.pureinkpress.com

In the era following the shift from a "flat Earth" to
a "round Earth," maps became invaluable.

Today, we undergo a profound revelation that
consciousness expands into infinity.

Our round Earth now holds boundless possibilities! The practices
of now are the maps guiding us through this vast awareness,
offering masterful greatness to all, not just the masters.

Illuminate the trails ahead — Be the light.

INSPIRED BY GURU SINGH

Contents

This book serves as my map, the one I wish I had years ago. It's dedicated to all the busy, no-BS truth seekers who work hard, play hard, and love hard—living their best life but still feeling that something is missing. It's for those ready to pause for a hot second, contemplate new ways of being, heal from the past, and reconnect to their ultimate health, happiness, and abundance!

Foreword

In a world overwhelmed by distractions and demands, where the clamor for our attention often stifles our inner peace, it's an honor to be among the first to experience this transformative guide.

Within the pages of *be. love.*, author, colleague, and dear friend, Christin Collins, shares the steps she has taken on her journey to self-discovery and healing. This book takes us beyond her inspirational memoir, *Her Phoenix Rising,* directly to the practical steps that can lead us to a life of improved health and happiness.

What distinguishes *be. love.* from similar offerings is Christin's authenticity. She has lived and breathed every lesson, revelation, and obstacle along her path through dedication, introspection, and self-care. She has created this resource as a gift for all walks of life, infused with insights applicable to both personal and professional life. Each chapter is meticulously crafted to be informative and transformative, presented in an easily digestible "how-to" format, complete with meaningful quotes, literary references, and practical tools. This is a roadmap toward sustainable success grounded in compassion, practicality, and love.

be. love. serves as a powerful reminder that at the core of every endeavor and aspiration lies the essence of connection—to oneself, family, friends, and colleagues. This book is a guiding compass that leads us toward greater health and the realization of our fullest potential—a must-have addition to every bookshelf or bedside table.

Thank you, Christin, for shining your light!

Be well. Stay inspired.

Scott Kashman, MHA, FACHE,
President/CEO, Healthcare Executive

Introduction

We are a disconnected culture, and it's destroying our health and well-being!

This awareness took me over fifty years to realize, and while I'm still on a journey to deeper understanding, I have landed on a plateau of reflection.

Do I know anyone who hasn't been broken at some point in their life?
Is it even possible to feel complete and truly happy?

I've spent my life searching for anything and everything outside of myself to make me feel whole and healthy. As the years passed, the joy derived from each alteration in my lifestyle or mind-blowing achievement diminished rapidly. Heck, it got to the point where I found myself barely completing one endeavor before plunging into the next, chasing the promised dopamine hit of a fresh pursuit.

I was happily married with two great stepkids and was in relatively good shape as a vegan triathlete. I also had a thriving career as a healthcare executive, which provided me with the means to enjoy life's finer things. Even with all that, as I approached fifty, a realization dawned on me—I wasn't truly satisfied. Despite all my best efforts, my health report showed an off-the-chart inflammation score, prompting me to question: *What am I missing?*

Over the years, my body issued numerous warning signs. The relentless presence of irritable bowel syndrome and chronic inflammation became a daily ordeal, reaching its zenith around 2 p.m. each day when my midsection would invariably bloat, resembling a seven-month pregnancy. I resorted to concealing this transformation under loose-fitting clothes, grappling with frustration, fear, and sadness over not being able to figure out what I was doing wrong. Along with the unexplained bloating, I'd also have random skin irritations appear overnight, which were, of course, resilient to treatments with any topical creams and steroids. My exhaustion was palpable, yet I powered through each hectic day fueled by caffeine, Diet Coke, sheer will, and perseverance. I attributed these struggles to the inevitable toll of aging.

In hindsight, I've dealt with skin and digestive issues for as long as I can remember. I was diagnosed with ovarian cancer at the age of twenty-one and underwent aggressive treatment to thankfully cure that. Two intestinal resections were followed by a lupus diagnosis, and the subsequent list of autoimmune conditions that ensued was extensive.

In my memoir, *Her Phoenix Rising*, I share my oftentimes awkward and thick-headed experiences toward overcoming my physical challenges once and for all. This is when I discovered that the root cause of *dis*-ease is often not something a hospital test can pinpoint. I had been sexually abused for a large part of my childhood, and I had a number of other heartbreaking challenges, as many of us do. Although I went to therapy and thought I had put all that behind me, my body told a different story.

Since then, I've learned that trauma can function as a switch, reshaping the blueprints of our bodies and resulting in imbalances that may manifest into different illnesses. Traumas affecting our health can vary greatly in nature and intensity, and an experience that strongly affects one person may not affect another in the same way.

Am I here to perpetuate the stories of my past traumas, giving them energy to live on? Absolutely not. We all carry wounds from past experiences. Dragging around unhealed trauma is exhausting and detrimental to our emotional, mental, physical, and spiritual well-being. It creates barriers that keep us stuck. Moreover, it prevents us from fully enjoying the present moment, often leading to disconnection or dissociation.

Over the years, I've noticed this behavior manifesting in various ways in my own life—either through excessive shopping, overconsumption of alcohol to numb the present moment, or my tendency to judge everyone and everything around me in an attempt to control my surroundings for a false sense of safety. Eventually, I realized I hadn't fully healed from my early traumas. Instead, I dissociated from them and built walls around my heart. I painstakingly created environments where my triggers would be avoided at all costs. It was utterly and completely exhausting! I was missing out on truly living my life.

Wake-up calls can manifest in various ways; for me, it was ill health. For you, the circumstances may be entirely different from mine, yet you might still find yourself in the same emotional state as me when your wake-up call arrives—*empty.*

I didn't arrive at empty right away. The more I sat and contemplated, the more the word *empty* bubbled up. I had built an incredible life on top of and in spite of my disconnect. As I reflected, I realized this exhaustive energy to constantly pursue some ever-moving target of wholeness was my attempt to deny what was truly inside.

How do we take that first step off the hamster wheel of constant human *doing* and learn how to pay attention to our bodies, our minds, our relationships, and our lives? How do we become a human *being*?

How do we slow down enough to investigate what is creating our disconnect within ourselves and with the world around us? How do we step toward living a purposeful life of optimal health, happiness, and well-being?

Let me get straight to the point. I often struggle to complete books, courses, or workshops because I lose interest. Many authors tend to over-explain or overstate. If you're anything like me, you prefer a direct approach, bullet-pointing straight to the conclusion.

To attain health, happiness, abundance—or anything else you desire—you must turn within. Seeking external sources will never lead to satiation and wholeness.

The answers we're looking for are already here, inside us. They are divinely different and distinctive for each of us. All we need to do is stop spinning, sit still in the moment, and reconnect with who we are and why we are here.

Our recent collective experiences during the global pandemic served as a catalyst for many of us to awaken. As a community, we have forgotten. Forgotten our unique, divine, individual purposes for being alive. We've neglected the fact that we are interconnected—to our higher selves, to one another, to Mother Nature, and to every beautiful living thing that surrounds us. We are conscious beings, and consciousness is infinite!

The answers we're searching for are already inside us, regardless of the obstacles in our way. We have the tools to find balance. We always have. In the pages of this book, I hope to inspire an awakening within you of what you already know.

It's time to remember.

It's time to shine your light out into the world as a beacon for others to do the same.

It's time to—*be. love.*

PART ONE

Root Cause Compass

The darker the night, the
brighter your stars will shine.

THE CORNERSTONES OF HEALING

Trauma

"I am not what happened to me,
I am what I choose to become."
— CARL JUNG

In the complexity of our lives, we all carry scars, some more apparent than others.

There are those significant blows, the "Big Ts," recognized by professionals as events that can reshape our very core. These typically large-scale events, such as natural disasters or severe abuse, have a deep and immediate effect on our mental and emotional well-being, often requiring extensive therapeutic intervention to heal.

Then there are the subtler wounds, the "Little Ts," weaving their way into the framework of our being, quietly influencing our growth. These often more nuanced experiences can be caused by things like bullying, emotional neglect, or microaggressions. While they may not seem as overtly distressing, these experiences can still have a significant cumulative effect over time, gradually shaping our beliefs, behaviors, and relationships.

Both types of traumas, whether "Big Ts" or "Little Ts," are important to recognize and address, as they can greatly impact our lives and shape our adult selves.

Bearing the weight of unresolved trauma takes a toll on every aspect of our well-being—emotionally, mentally, physically, and spiritually. Like formidable obstacles, these unresolved issues create barriers, hindering our personal growth. Facing the past can be a daunting task, often leading us to subconsciously avoid the present moment when it reminds us of associated pains. I have certainly found comfort in disconnection and avoidance.

As a survivor of overwhelming childhood trauma—a Big T survivor—the scars run deep. Years of therapy provided a measure of healing, but approaching fifty unveiled the realization for me that more work lay ahead. It was a moment of introspection, prompting a pause, reflection, and a shift in my perspective. They say the definition of insanity is repeating the same patterns and expecting different results. It was time for a shift in my approach to healing.

An epiphany of how to view a *root cause* trauma revealed itself to me when I read Michael Singer's *Untethered Soul*. This impactful book provided fireworks of wisdom, helping me to understand how trauma works.

One of my favorite parts was the story of having a thorn in our arm, to represent a trauma in our lives. Singer asks us to imagine the thorn pressing against a nerve, and every time it's touched, it causes us a lot of pain. Sleeping is difficult because you might roll onto it. Getting close to others is hard because they might touch it. It makes life a constant struggle, leaving you with only two possible choices to alleviate the agony.[1]

These two choices boil down to: one, constructing an entire existence around your thorn to shield it from any touch, or two, removing the thorn.

As simple as it may seem to extract the thorn, the process is not as straightforward as it appears. Our minds have an effective built-in mechanism of protection, which often shields us subconsciously from our root cause issue, making it challenging to address. Though I believed I had removed my thorn many times, my efforts were in vain. My subconscious defenses were always at work, masking my healing through avoidance of genuine connection. For me, the thorn evolved into a pervasive force dictating every aspect of my life.

What a revelation! I had unknowingly built an entire existence around my deep-seated trauma, including the steel trap around my heart. The stress from the subconscious energy I put into keeping my pain dormant was actually making me sick. It also kept me from truly feeling all that life had to offer.

It was time for me to put what I was doing on *pause* and tap into my innate wisdom to *remove* and *release* my trauma. It was time to truly live, thrive, and be well.

For me, that journey started with: *Forgiveness.*

Forgiveness

"To forgive is to set a prisoner free and
discover that the prisoner was you."
— LEWIS B. SMEDES

In the immense potential of the human heart, forgiveness emerges as a transformative force capable of mending the deepest wounds and liberating the spirit. It is an adventure that begins within, navigating the intricate terrain of emotions, grudges, and the arduous process of letting go.

Forgiveness is not a concession but an empowering choice, a deliberate act of reclaiming one's inner peace. It is a sacred dance between the self and the world, possessing the power to transform pain into wisdom and healing.

Releasing and forgiving those who had hurt me were not acts of condoning what had occurred; the abuse was deplorable and always will be. Forgiveness, however, released me from the past, allowing me to live in the present while showing compassion for my perpetrator.

This act energetically cut the cord that held me to my thorn and freed me from dragging my root cause ball and chain everywhere.

I believe we are all interconnected; we are all one. Wasting energy hating another is only hurting oneself. Instead, when we can release with love, we free ourselves from our trauma prisons.

In my process of forgiveness, what took me the longest to figure out was how to forgive *myself.* The shame I unknowingly carried for not speaking up, for not finding safety, for not knowing how to navigate such hell as a young child weighed heavily on me. I had no idea I was carrying that shame. I only knew that I felt gross, used, and unworthy of love. With the help of professionals, I returned to that young girl living inside of me and hugged her. Holding her hand, I apologized for my youthful innocence. Together, we could step forward whole and complete, knowing that our traumatic experience was part of our path, making us wiser, stronger, and more compassionate.

As I continued to pursue my healing and well-being, I uncovered deeper layers to the intricacies of trauma. I've learned that in addition to carrying traumas from our early childhood, we can also experience something known as generational transference.

Generational transference explores the reflective idea that our cells carry imprints of the struggles, injustices, and traumas experienced by our forebears in both past generations and previous lives. This concept emerges from a synthesis of scientific exploration and metaphysical understanding, suggesting that the impact of historical adversities can linger within the very makeup of our being. Epigenetic changes, as explored in the book *What Happened to You* by Oprah Winfrey and Dr. Bruce D. Perry, illuminate how these imprints are stored within our cellular makeup, waiting to be passed down to subsequent generations.

Winfrey and Perry write, *"Go back a few centuries and imagine a young man captured in Africa, brutally enslaved, shackled, starved, transported by a slave ship to a life of bondage filled with loss, violence, and multiple forms of trauma. Surviving such extreme, multiple, and ongoing traumas— as missions of remarkable human beings did—would likely create a cascade of adaptive changes all the way down to the regulation of gene expression. It is likely that, over the generations, in different environments, once-adaptive changes would become maladaptive."*[2]

Recognizing generational transference prompts contemplation on the interconnectedness of our familial and ancestral histories, shaping our physical characteristics and influencing our emotional and psychological well-being. It underscores the importance of understanding our lineage, not just as a source of pride or identity but as a reservoir of potential healing. Unraveling the threads of generational trauma can then become an essential aspect of the forgiveness journey, allowing us to address our personal wounds as well as those etched into the very blueprint of our cellular makeup.

By acknowledging and releasing these imprints with compassion, we embark on a path toward healing not just for ourselves, but for the generations that came before and those that will follow. We can then break the chains of generational suffering, paving the way for a more liberated and harmonious existence.

On every level, forgiveness becomes the key that unlocks the door to the gift hidden in plain sight. More than an act of absolution for others, it is a thoughtful gesture of self-love and self-liberation. When we release the grip of past traumas, whether personal or ancestral, we can step into the present with newfound clarity and resilience. It becomes an empowering embrace of our humanity, and in this moment of grace, we unearth the seed of our *purpose*, patiently awaiting our acknowledgment and nurturing.

Purpose

---

*"The two most important days in your life are the day
you are born and the day you find out why."*

— MARK TWAIN

What propels you out of bed each day? What ignites your passion, evoking a smile or a boundless sense of joy? Why do you matter? These questions emerged for me amid numerous personal and professional accomplishments that failed to bring a sense of true fulfillment or satisfaction. It was at this juncture, I dug into the concept of purpose and the vital significance of connecting with it.

As author and spiritual teacher Eckhart Tolle writes in his transformational book, *A New Earth*, *"As soon as you rise above mere survival, the question of meaning and purpose becomes of paramount importance in your life."*[3]

Understanding and connecting with our purpose is indeed of great importance. I believe that each of us possesses a unique, divine reason for being here, a distinct purpose beyond mere existence. We are here to undergo an experience and bring it to fruition. Aligning with the individual essence of our life's purpose allows us to tap into our fullest potential, transcending the notion that our professional endeavors must solely define our purpose. Instead, our purpose radiates through every facet of our existence, influencing everything we undertake. Living on purpose embodies the distinctive "why" of our lives, offering the tranquility and fluidity essential for a vibrant, purposeful life.

Frequently, life's purpose emerges from the skills and strengths cultivated or inherited through generations—a kind of passing of the torch. However, even more commonly, purpose is shaped by the transformative power of trauma. Our traumas, or *root causes*, often act as unexpected teachers, guiding us toward discovering our ultimate purpose. The wounds we bear, whether from personal experiences or the echoes of generational struggles, become the forge for crafting resilience, compassion, and wisdom, unveiling unique gifts that lie dormant within us.

Having navigated the depths of trauma, I've noticed that I carry an inexplicable drive that strongly shapes my life. Whether through acts of kindness, mentorship, or pursuing a career dedicated to a higher cause, fulfilling my purpose has been a powerful force in my subconscious. Only when I finally embraced that drive and embarked on the process of writing my first book, did I truly comprehend my purpose—to inspire awakening, starting with self!

Although I didn't fully grasp this realization immediately, I unmistakably felt a sense of home from those six simple words. Operating from this reflective awareness has since allowed me to navigate the currents of my life with more ease.

The importance of purpose has transcended cultures worldwide throughout history, exemplified by the Japanese concept known as *ikigai*, which translates to "that which makes life worth living." *Ikigai* gained prominence through Dan Buettner's groundbreaking Blue Zones research and documentary series.

At its essence, *ikigai* involves identifying sources of joy and fulfillment, placing emphasis on personal passions and interests. This dimension aligns with the idea of doing what you love, offering another perspective on the foundational principle of embracing one's purpose; it's the driving force that motivates individuals every morning to get out of bed, even at the glorious age of one hundred. It serves as a key to a long and fulfilling life, prompting deeper reflections on personal values and contributions within your community.

Ultimately, a life infused with purpose is a life well lived. It is the quiet whisper that calls us to align our actions with our values, cultivate a meaningful existence, and leave an indelible mark on the world. A world that, regardless of who you are, where you live, or what philosophies you hold, will always come down to one thing—love.

The ultimate purpose of life is to know itself as love!

Gratitude

---

*"Gratitude makes sense of our past, brings peace
for today, and creates a vision for tomorrow."*
— MELODY BEATTIE

The energy of gratitude is a powerful force that permeates every aspect of our lives, influencing our thoughts, emotions, and actions. At its core, gratitude is our deep appreciation for the blessings, gifts, and experiences that enrich our lives, big and small. It's our acknowledgment of the goodness surrounding us and our recognition of the abundance flowing through every moment.

When I cultivate an attitude of gratitude, I shift my focus from what is lacking to what is present. Instead of dwelling on my problems or shortcomings, I choose to direct my attention to the countless blessings I often take for granted. This shift in perspective opens my heart and mind to the richness of life, fostering a sense of contentment, peace, and joy.

Gratitude is a powerful emotion that has captured the attention of researchers across various fields because of its profound effects on human well-being. It has also greatly impacted my outlook on life. It's a journey that began for me during the painful divorce of my short-lived first marriage. At that time, the idea of gratitude felt foreign to me. How could I find anything to be thankful for when my world was crumbling around me? However, as I probed deeper into the practice of being grateful, I began to realize that gratitude wasn't about denying my struggles; it was about finding light in the darkness. I started small, focusing on simple blessings like the warmth of the sun on my face and the laughter of a loved one. With each expression of gratitude, I felt a subtle shift within me—a flicker of hope. Over time, I began to discover the transformative power of gratitude.

Within my career, I've discovered compelling evidence of how gratitude influences psychological well-being, physiological health, and social connections. Numerous studies underscore the insightful effects of gratitude on mental well-being and consistently link it to heightened happiness, increased life satisfaction, and a brighter overall mood. Moreover, individuals who regularly express gratitude tend to experience lower levels of stress, anxiety, and depression, as well as lower blood pressure, enhanced immune function, improved sleep quality, and a reduced risk of chronic illnesses.

The impact of gratitude extends to interpersonal relationships as well. When we express gratitude toward others, it strengthens bonds, fosters a sense of closeness, and encourages prosocial behavior. Over time, with consistent gratitude practice, we can fortify neural pathways linked to positive emotions and overall well-being.

As author Marc Reklau says in his book, *The Life-Changing Power of Gratitude*, *"Gratitude is one of the most powerful forces in the universe, and being grateful not only brings good things into our lives but also makes us notice more and more of those things that are already there. And when I talk about practicing gratitude, I don't talk about practicing it once a year or every now and then. I talk about practicing it every single day and throughout each day. Make gratitude a lifestyle."* [4]

Gratitude has inspired me to pay it forward, motivating acts of kindness, generosity, and altruism toward others. By extending gratitude beyond words to meaningful actions, I contribute positively to my community and the world around me.

My exploration into the science of gratitude has been transformative, reshaping my outlook on life and enhancing my overall well-being. As I continue to explore the depths of being grateful for both the "good" things and seemingly "bad" (which I feel is just a limited perspective), I've discovered a source of happiness, health, and social connection inspired by the endless possibilities it holds for enriching my life and the lives of those around me.

No healing process is complete without gratitude!

PART TWO

be. love. GPS

b	breathe
e	emotions
.	pause
l	let go
o	open heart
v	visualize
e	energize
.	prioritize

be. love.

"Your task is not to seek for love, but merely to seek and find all the barriers within yourself that you have built against it."

— RUMI

What does it mean to *be. love.?*

be. love. encapsulates the idea of embodying love in all aspects of one's life. It means approaching oneself, others, and the world with compassion, kindness, understanding, and empathy. Being love involves acting from a place of unconditional acceptance and generosity, nurturing meaningful connections, and fostering a sense of unity and interconnectedness with all beings. It's about radiating positivity, spreading joy, and making a positive difference in the lives of others through loving actions, words, and intentions. Ultimately, to *be. love.* is a thoughtful commitment to embodying the highest qualities of the heart and sharing them with the world.

We are all born with the innate knowing and natural instinct of being love, but as our human lives unfold, our experiences and traumas often lead us farther away from that knowing. We lose our natural connection to ourselves, and for many of us, life becomes an adventure to find our way back to self.

In the quest back to self, we strive to rediscover our true essence. This odyssey reconnects us with our inner wisdom of self-love and acceptance. It represents a return to love, a personal and profound exploration for each of us, shaped by our unique experiences and biases, molding our individual realities into intrinsic truths. At the heart of our personal narratives beats a shared resonance gently guiding us home.

Numerous pathways exist to lead us back to ourselves, a realization I've embraced within my journey. Each route that has guided me toward healing holds a special place in my experience, and this abundance of paths is equally accessible to you on your life's voyage.

Throughout my ongoing exploration, I've adopted a simple yet significant routine that helps me find clarity when facing a crossroad. This practice has enabled me to realize that the path consistently leading to my feelings of wholeness is always anchored in one thing—love.

Grounding ourselves in the present and reconnecting with love initiates a substantial reprogramming of forgotten subconscious patterns. Approaching this exploration with curiosity and wonder unlocks the mysteries of both our conscious and subconscious being. It's time to let our *super*conscious higher self, also known as our unwavering anchor in the shared oneness with all beings, guide us on our transformative journeys.

Healing tools need not be complicated or expensive; they reside within each of us—for free.

Let's surrender to the essence of being and reconnect with the boundless energy of *love!*

> *"Love is the bridge between you and everything."*
>
> — RUMI

breathe

"Breath is the bridge which connects life to consciousness, which unites your body to your thoughts. Whenever your mind becomes scattered, use your breath as the means to take hold of your mind again."

— THICH NHAT HANH

The present moment—here and now—how's it going for you? Are you fully present? Do you know how to truly live in the moment?

Many masters of well-being assert that the pathway to reconnecting with ourselves, fostering healing, thriving, and achieving overall well-being is by immersing in the present moment. To accomplish this, we must momentarily halt the whirlwind of life around us and learn how to simply *breathe*.

I firmly believe that breathing is the vital bedrock of life—not merely for the obvious reason that without it, we would not exist, but because it serves as a bridge to wholeness and forms the foundation for all experiences in the human condition. While harnessing the benefits of properly breathing might sound simple initially, it took me years to grasp its vitality. For as long as I can remember, I'd often find myself in situations where I'd be uptight and shallow-breathing my way through the past or dissociatively daydreaming about terraforming my future. Being in the *now* was only a state that author Eckhart Tolle purported. It couldn't really be all that important, could it?

The answer to that question dawned on me during a long-awaited vacation to a destination I had dreamt of for years. While I observed others holding hands, laughing, and lounging in hammocks by the pool, I found myself consumed with planning the next destination on my bucket list—right there in the lobby of paradise! Despite being in a fantastic place, I struggled to fully enjoy the moment. Which was baffling! It became evident that I had a problem: I couldn't embrace the present. Perhaps I was avoiding feeling it? My heart felt closed off, leaving me unable to engage with the here and now.

Upon returning home after that revelation, I decided to try my hand at yoga, thinking it might help me be present. To say it was a struggle would be putting it mildly—poor yoga instructor. I'd fidget uncontrollably, unable to relax and simply breathe. Then came this thing called "meditation." Seriously? Who has time to sit on the floor and not think? My stress levels soared as I worried about all the things I should be doing instead of sitting there thinking about nothing. How was that supposed to help me?

Stubborn as I am, I didn't give up on figuring out meditation. I placed a notepad and pen by my side. When urgent thoughts popped into my head, I'd jot them down and return to my attempt to be in the present moment. I tried free meditation apps, sitting on a blanket, covering my lap with a blanket, lying down, doing it when I woke up or before bed, outside on the dock, upstairs in the guest room. Nothing seemed to make this *being in the here and now* thing any easier for me.

Slowly, and I mean slowly, I managed to sit for longer periods. I exclusively focused on the actual sound of taking a deep breath in, then gently exhaling. I associated that sound with being in a state of love for that moment, for my surroundings and for myself. In the beginning, two minutes of meditation felt nearly impossible. However, once I had something concrete to concentrate on—my breath and the love surrounding me—I found myself being able to sit for longer. I progressed from two minutes to three, then ten, twelve, and even fifteen minutes!

Sitting started to feel luxurious, and I observed a heightened sense of calm throughout my day.

Others began to notice. I was less snappy and less reactive, and I wasn't rushing to fill void spaces like I used to. This newfound calmness extended to my friendships, family relationships, and even the dynamic, large healthcare system environment where I worked, capturing the attention of my boss, Scott. Accustomed to my fiery reactions, Scott was taken aback when a potentially upsetting meeting failed to elicit my usual tirade. A newfound sense of calm enveloped me, and, sensing the anomaly, Scott cautiously inquired about my well-being. "Hey, are you okay with all the changes they're requesting here?"

Instead of responding immediately, I took a moment to inhale deeply and contemplate what had just happened from a place of love. Then, with clarity, I responded, "It's definitely unexpected, but I'm sure if we all work on it this week, it'll get sorted quickly."

Perplexed by my uncharacteristic answer, he probed further. "You're unusually calm. I'm not used to seeing that. There's something up. What is it?"

Surprised that he noticed, I admitted to my efforts at meditation. Despite his initial disbelief that I could, in fact, sit still long enough to incorporate the long-held practice from life masters of the past, Scott, being a class act, acknowledged the change in me.

My calmness had a ripple effect. A month later, inspired by our conversation, Scott attempted meditation himself. Not one for sitting still, he found his meditative haven in running, a revelation he shared with a mix of pride and humor. As the months unfolded, the undeniable calm in Scott's demeanor became palpable, showcasing the effectiveness of his unconventional yet profoundly significant version of presence, all sparked by witnessing the shift in me.

Undoubtedly, each of us approaches *being in the now* in our own unique way. Whether sitting in the lotus position with closed eyes, running a marathon, as in Scott's case, or engaging in anything in between. Grounding ourselves in the present and taking a moment to breathe is fundamental to our health and well-being. Being present can calm our nervous system, lower blood pressure (after getting the hang of it!), and make us less reactive, more contemplative, and simply more pleasant to be around.

Beyond its ability to center us in the present moment, conscious breathing boasts incredible foundational health benefits. No wonder it feels so good! Breathing directly influences our immune systems, weight, circulation, mood, sexual function, and longevity. In his *New York*

Times best-selling book, *Breath*, James Nestor guides readers through an exploration of the diverse blessings of connecting with breath.

"Researchers have shown that many modern maladies... could either be reduced or reversed simply by changing the way we inhale and exhale... No matter what we eat, how much we exercise, how resilient our genes are, how skinny or young or wise we are – none of it will matter unless we're breathing correctly. The missing pillar in health is breath. It all starts there."[5]

Breath is also an intricate part of Dr. Deepak Chopra's work. In his book *Metahuman*, we learn that our current culture and lifestyle create a continued state of acute stress, while reconnecting with breath brings our body back to a state of balance and relieves tension.

"In modern life, being in a state of chronic low-level stress is so common as to be accepted as normal. But your body doesn't experience it as normal at all; the earliest beginnings of heart disease, hypertension, sleep, and digestive disorders, and probably some cancers can be traced to chronic stress. Vagal breathing brings the state of the body back into balance and relieves tension."[6]

I believe that breathing serves as a bridge between our physical existence and the realm of love and spirit. By harnessing the power of the breath, we can deepen our connection to love, embody its essence, and infuse every aspect of our being with its transformative energy.

Right *now* is the only moment in life that we truly possess. The past is behind us, and much of what lies ahead will only be a reflection of what we are doing and feeling today. So, why not make *now* count? Let's find our breath, follow its flow, express gratitude for it, and allow it to wash over our bodies and souls. By calming our nervous systems and replenishing our cells, we pave the way for optimal health, happiness, and abundance.

And it all begins with something as simple as *breathing*.

BREATHING EXERCISE

1. **Find a Comfortable Seated Position:** You can sit on a chair with your feet flat on the floor or cross-legged on a cushion.

2. **Gently Straighten Your Spine:** Allow your shoulders to relax. Rest your hands on your knees or in your lap.

3. **Close Your Eyes Softly:** Minimize external distractions.

4. **Take a Deep Breath:** Inhale slowly and deeply through your nose. Feel your lungs expanding, filling with air. Count silently to four as you breathe in.

5. **Hold the Breath:** At the top of your inhale, briefly hold your breath for a count of two. Allow yourself to be present in this moment of stillness.

6. **Exhale Slowly:** Release the breath slowly and completely through your mouth. Again, count to four as you exhale.

7. **Pause:** At the end of your exhale, pause for another count of two. Experience the emptiness before the next breath.

8. **Repeat:** Continue this rhythmic breathing pattern. Inhale for four counts, hold for two, exhale for four counts, and pause for two. Allow your breath to become a steady and calming anchor.

9. **Mindful Awareness:** If your mind starts to wander, gently bring your focus back to the sensation of your breath. Imagine that your breath is pure love entering every cell of your body with each inhale.

10. **End with Gratitude:** After a few minutes, gradually return to natural breathing. Open your eyes and take a moment to acknowledge the stillness and love within. Express gratitude for this time you've dedicated to your well-being.

Feel free to adjust the counts or the duration based on your comfort level or situation.*

---

* To access this exercise/meditation online, please visit www.christincollins.com.

"The more you listen to your breath, the more you can hear the voice of your soul."

— MA JAYA SATI BHAGAVATI

emotions

"The more adept you become at being fully present for your emotions, the more quickly you'll find the relief of release. Feelings are like the weather, constantly changing and, with a little time and acknowledgement, blowing through."
— CY WAKEMAN, *Life's Messy, Live Happy*

Now that we've sown the seeds of being present in the moment and reconnecting with our breath, what do we do when emotions and thoughts arise that we may not be eager to confront?

Grief ~ Fear ~ Vulnerability ~ Anger ~ Shame ~ Loneliness ~ Sadness ~ Guilt ~ Anxiety

What about positive emotions that we can't process fully?

Joy ~ Love ~ Gratitude ~ Contentment ~ Hope ~ Satisfaction ~ Amusement ~ Excitement ~ Pride

As I continued to better understand the connection between mind and body, I noticed a significant blind spot—I was out of touch with my emotions. Except for anger, that is, I was rather exceptional at feeling that one.

Every day, we all experience a range of human emotions, which I have learned provide us with valuable insights into our lives. Popular author and spiritual teacher, Esther Hicks (a.k.a. Abraham Hicks), discusses the concept of our Emotional Guidance System in her book, *The Astonishing Power of Emotions.*

Esther teaches that our emotions serve as a guidance system, indicating whether our thoughts and actions are in alignment with our true desires and well-being. The teachings emphasize the importance of paying attention to our emotions as a means of navigating life and making choices that lead to joy and fulfillment.[7] When we dismiss or suppress our emotions, we face disconnection from our well-being, ultimately leading to a state of *dis*harmony and *dis*ease within.

Another intriguing perspective on how emotions can actually be stored in our bodies and impact our health emerges from the ancient Eastern philosophy of the chakra system. Our chakras provide a framework that intricately weaves together our emotions, energy, and overall well-being. Consisting of seven spinning energy wheels positioned along the spine, each chakra is linked to specific facets of our physical, emotional, and spiritual selves. These energetic hubs act as conduits for the vital life force energy, or "prana," shaping our emotional landscape and influencing the ebb and flow of our feelings. In essence, understanding and harmonizing these chakras becomes a gateway to emotional balance, fostering a deep connection between our inner emotional realms and the broader scope of mind, body, and spirit.

I've found this ideology particularly interesting in regard to my childhood trauma. The first chakra, or *root chakra*, caught my attention as it plays a crucial role in shaping our sense of stability, security, and how we connect to the real world. It also addresses basic survival needs like food, shelter, and safety. In terms of physical health, this chakra influences the vitality of our bodies, and any imbalances may manifest as ailments, particularly in the lower part of the body.

Additionally, the root chakra is intricately linked to our primal instincts, influencing our responses to challenges through the fight-or-flight mechanism. It extends its influence to our roots, connecting us with family, ancestors, and a sense of belonging, with imbalances often tied to family dynamics and ancestral patterns.[8]

Wow! Translated, to me, this meant that my childhood sexual abuse—my *root cause*—disrupted the energy and flow of my *root chakra,* a disruption that may have led to potentially all my core health issues, mostly located in the lower part of my abdomen. Ovarian cancer and bowel issues, which in turn affected my skin issues and constant state of fight or flight, leading to inflammation. Did I say wow? Irrespective of what my belief system may be, I couldn't ignore the potential significance of this information. Traditional medical approaches yielded no relief for too many years, what harm was there in considering this idea as a possibility?

Exploring this perspective brought numerous facets of my life into focus. It made me contemplate how many of us have actually felt sensations within our bodies when we've actively tried to suppress a strong emotion. I can see now that when emotions are suppressed, the body becomes a container, subtly absorbing the unexpressed feelings like a sponge. Tension might settle in the shoulders, a heaviness may engulf the chest, or knots could form in the stomach. The body, intricate in its communication, becomes a repository for the emotions we resist expressing. The sensations might linger, serving as a quiet reminder that our emotional experiences are not separate from our physical being.

Having worked in the executive medical realm, I'm acutely aware that science has increasingly recognized the significant impact of emotions on overall health and well-being, emphasizing the importance of acknowledging and allowing oneself to feel a spectrum of emotions. When emotions are stifled or suppressed, the body can respond with increased stress levels, leading to the release of stress hormones like cortisol. Prolonged stress, in turn, has been linked to various health issues, including cardiovascular problems, compromised immune function, and inflammatory responses.

Allowing ourselves to genuinely feel and express emotions is proven to have positive effects on both mental and physical health. It improves mood, reduces stress, and increases psychological resilience. Through my journey, I've come to appreciate that acknowledging and embracing a range of emotions, even those we label as negative, contributes significantly to emotional intelligence and overall well-being. Navigating and dealing with emotions effectively requires a multifaceted approach—one that acknowledges their presence, allows for expression, and encourages the development of healthy coping mechanisms.

For me, first and foremost, self-awareness became my cardinal direction. It's been a game-changer in my healing. Tuning into and identifying my emotions helps lay the groundwork for understanding their roots and significance. Mindfulness practices, particularly meditation and deep-breathing exercises, are my trusty sidekicks, guiding me to cultivate self-awareness by anchoring me in the present moment.

Once we recognize our emotions, acceptance can take the spotlight. It's crucial to embrace the truth that feeling a mix of emotions, both positive and negative, is a natural part of being human. I've learned firsthand that suppressing or brushing aside my emotions often leads to inner turmoil, heightened stress, and illness. Now, I make a conscious effort to explore constructive outlets for expressing my emotions—whether it's opening up to a trusted friend, pouring my thoughts into a journal, seeking counseling from a mental health professional, or finding solace in being outdoors. These are all signs of strength, not weakness.

Equally important to me is building a repertoire of healthy coping strategies such as regular physical activity, maintaining a balanced diet, and ensuring adequate sleep. Developing resilience and adaptive coping mechanisms enables all of us to navigate life's challenges and emotions with greater ease.

As shared by Neale Donald Walsh in *Book One* of *Conversations with God*, *"Feeling is the language of the soul. If you want to know what's true for you about something, look at how you're feeling about it. Feelings are sometimes difficult to acknowledge, yet hidden in your deepest feeling is your highest truth."*[9]

So, we are here to *feel* our emotions. All of them. In real time. Breathe them in, breathe them out, and release them. Be curious about them. Try them on, see if they feel right. Let's use them to help us decide who we want to be, who we are, and who we are not. Our highest truth remains consistent for all of us. It's the destination we aim for, regardless of the challenges we've encountered. And that universal truth is—love!

EMOTIONS EXERCISE

1. **Awareness:** Find a quiet and comfortable space. Close your eyes and take a few deep breaths. Allow yourself to become fully present in the moment.

2. **Identify the Emotion:** Bring to mind a situation or thought that is causing you emotional discomfort. Without judgment, name the emotion you're feeling. It might be sadness, anger, fear, joy, or any other emotion.

3. **Body Scan:** Pay attention to how this emotion is manifesting in your body. Are there any physical sensations? Tension in your shoulders, tightness in your chest, or a knot in your stomach? Scan your body from head to toe, noting any areas of tension or ease.

4. **Breath Awareness:** Shift your focus to your breath. Take slow, deliberate breaths. Notice the rhythm and depth of your breath. Use your breath to bring a sense of calm and grounding.

5. **Explore the Root Cause:** Without judgment, inquire about the root cause of the emotion. Is it related to a specific event, a thought pattern, or an expectation? Allow yourself to sit with this awareness without immediately seeking a solution.

6. **Acceptance:** Embrace the emotion without resisting it. Accept that emotions are a natural part of the human experience. Allow yourself to feel without attaching judgment to the emotion.

7. **Express or Release:** Depending on the nature of the emotion, consider expressing it in a healthy way. This could involve journaling, talking to a friend, or engaging in a physical activity. Alternatively, if the emotion is heavy, visualize releasing it with each exhale, letting it dissipate.

8. **Self-Compassion:** Offer yourself love and compassion. Understand that it's okay to feel a range of emotions. Treat yourself with the same love and kindness you would offer a friend going through a similar experience. Surround yourself in love. You are love!

9. **Express Gratitude:** Conclude the exercise by bringing to mind something you're grateful for. Gratitude can help shift your focus and bring a positive perspective.

Remember, this exercise is a tool for self-awareness and emotional well-being. Feel free to adapt it to suit your needs and preferences.*

---

* To access this exercise/meditation online, please visit www.christincollins.com.

> *"Emotions are like waves. You can't stop them from coming, but you can choose which ones to surf."*
> — JONATAN MARTENSSON

_____

_____

_____

_____

_____

_____

_____

_____

_____

_____

_____

_____

pause

---

*"The best time for you to pause, reflect, and reset
is when you don't have time for it."*
— KAREN SALMANSOHN

For most of my adult existence, life has felt like a relentless race, a marathon of responsibilities and obligations with every day a landslide of tasks, demands, and the exhausting pursuit of goals. It wasn't until I stumbled upon the transformative practice of *pausing* that I discovered a momentous shift in how I navigate the rhythm of my reality. Learning to pause is akin to unlocking a secret door to a world of tranquility amid life's hustle.

I wish I had learned about pausing much earlier than I did, but "better late than never," as they say. For those of you to whom this idea may be new, pausing is not about stopping time or avoiding responsibilities; instead, it is about creating a sacred space within the continuum of our lives. It's the practice of temporarily releasing the grip of our obligations to grant ourselves the gift of introspection. In moments of pause, we reconnect with our breath, the beating of our hearts, and the essence of our being.

This art requires a conscious effort to disentangle from the demands of the external world and turn inward. It's a momentary retreat into the sanctuary of our thoughts, feelings, and sensations. As we accept the stillness, we become attuned to the subtle nuances of our inner landscape.

The concept of pausing and actively listening landed on my radar when an unexpected opportunity presented itself. My husband, David, and I were tuned into *The Rich Roll Podcast*, a weekly valuable resource for us as we pursued wellness. Roll featured a diverse array of guests who helped us better understand ourselves and take control of our health. On this particular episode, Roll hosted Ryan Holiday, a master of stoicism, talking about his book, *Stillness Is the Key*. Holiday probed into the lives of individuals throughout history who had to make life-altering decisions by embracing the present moment.

Holiday shared excerpts highlighting historical figures like Lincoln, Roosevelt, and Seneca—some well-known, others unfamiliar. The common thread binding these diverse characters was how they took an intentional pause at pivotal moments. Amid the chaos, they halted and listened to themselves and their inner intuition.

The story that really struck a chord with me was the account of John F. Kennedy and the Bay of Pigs Invasion. For a newly elected and young president, this invasion posed a critical global issue that would be a challenge for any leader to navigate. The pressure was on, with all eyes on President Kennedy as he assessed the situation and formulated a plan of action. Urgency permeated the air, and those around him encouraged rapid retaliation.

Ryan Holiday recounted the tale of Kennedy taking a different approach. Instead of rushing into a response, the president took his time to ponder and contemplate. He asked many questions and was noticeably calm despite the obvious stress of the situation. There was no arguing or finger-pointing and when things did get heated, Kennedy laughed it off, making a concerted effort to keep egos out of the discussions. He would even leave the room if he felt his presence was stifling his advisor's ability to speak honestly, allowing everyone the space to debate and brainstorm freely.[10]

This reflection resonated with me as I imagined myself in his shoes. Having the courage to be still and listen in such a frantic time of emergency is admirable. Reflecting on times when I have faced sudden situations, my instinct has often been to opt for swift, decisive action. Fortunately, the lives of our nation were never at risk!

The proverbial light bulb illuminated my mind. The advantages of pausing and actively listening to my inner thoughts or tuning into my surroundings sparked a newfound clarity. The beauty of pausing is in its simplicity and accessibility. It doesn't require a secluded retreat or elaborate ritual; it thrives in the ordinary moments of our lives. Whether it's sipping a cup of tea in solitude, taking a stroll in nature, or simply closing our eyes to savor a deep breath, these instances of pause weave serenity through our daily routines.

After *much* practice, I started actively listening in conversations with those I interacted with at work. I used to be terrible at listening. I always had so much to say and believed my share was more important than whatever the other person was in the middle of saying. Boy, has that perspective shifted.

To pause within discussions has since become a place for digestion and respectful contemplation for me. I started noticing the space that would occur when someone finished speaking, and I got comfortable with the discomfort that such a pause might have brought in the past. Overall, the willingness to just listen without funneling the share into an imperative response was freeing and educational. I began to feel comfortable with people seeing things differently than I did, and I no longer needed agreement or alignment to feel safe.

I brought this skill into my day-to-day routine and morning ritual. Instead of diving headfirst into the daily grind, I began to wake up a little earlier, allowing myself the luxury of sipping my coffee in quiet contemplation. The stillness of the early morning became my refuge, a sacred space where I could set the tone for the day ahead.

Nature became another ally in my process of pausing. I started to take regular walks, immersing myself in the symphony of waves hitting the shore, the chirping of birds, and the soothing sound of wind blowing through the trees. These moments of communion with nature became my reset button, a source of inspiration that grounded me in the present.

During the bustling workday, I introduced micro-pauses. Whether it was closing my eyes for a few deep breaths or gazing out of the window for a moment, these pauses became anchors that prevented me from getting swept away in the current of busyness.

As I adopted the practice of pausing, I noticed a transformation within. The constant background noise of stress and hurriedness began to fade, and it was replaced by a sense of calm and clarity. The art of pausing became a beacon, guiding me to navigate life with intentionality.

Now, the art of pausing has become an indispensable part of my daily life. It's a practice that continues to unfold, offering moments of reflection, gratitude, and the wisdom that comes from being present in the now.

In these pauses, I've discovered the true richness of life is not in its speed but in the depth of each mindful breath and the beauty found in the spaces in between. It beckons us to question the quality of our engagements, urging us to infuse intentionality into each action. It is an invitation to reclaim our moments from a place of love, one breath at a time.

THE POWER OF PAUSE EXERCISE

The art of pausing is a transformative practice that invites you to step back from the hustle and bustle of life, allowing moments of stillness and reflection. This exercise helps you integrate the power of pause into your daily routine, fostering a sense of presence and mindfulness.

You may notice at this point how each exercise builds on the previous exercises we've learned, helping you expand and explore as you go along.

1. **Find Your Pause Sanctuary:** Choose a space where you can be alone and undisturbed for a few minutes. It could be a corner in your home, a quiet park bench, or a cozy chair by a window. Ensure the environment promotes a sense of calm.

2. **Breathe:** Sit or stand comfortably. Close your eyes and take a few deep breaths. Inhale slowly through your nose, allowing your lungs to fill with air, and exhale gently through your mouth. Let each breath ground you in the present moment.

3. **Mindful Observation:** Open your eyes and take in your surroundings. Engage your senses. What do you see, hear, smell, or feel? Pay attention to the details— the play of light, the rustling of leaves, or the sensation of the ground beneath you.

4. **Body Scan:** Bring your awareness to your body. Starting from your toes, mentally scan each part, releasing any tension as you go. Notice how your body feels, and let go of any areas of tightness.

5. **Set an Intention:** Reflect on the purpose of this pause. What do you hope to gain? It could be clarity, peace, or simply a break from the routine. Write down a brief intention if you have a pen and paper.

6. **Silent Reflection:** Allow a few moments of silence. Let your mind settle. If thoughts arise, observe them without judgment and gently guide your focus back to the present—back to love. You are love!

7. **Express Gratitude:** Take a moment to acknowledge the positives in your life. What are you grateful for today? Express gratitude silently or jot down a few notes if you have a pen and paper.

8. **Closing the Pause:** When you feel ready, gently bring your attention to where you are. Take a deep breath, and if your eyes are closed, slowly open them. Recognize and embrace the transition from pause to the ongoing rhythm of your day.

9. **Incorporate Micro-Pauses:** Throughout your day, practice micro-pauses. Set a reminder to take one or two minutes for a mindful breath or an appreciative observation of your surroundings. These moments can be powerful anchors of pause amid daily activities.

10. **Reflection:** After completing the exercise, reflect on your experience. How did the pause make you feel? Did you notice any shifts in your mindset or energy levels? Consider regularly integrating moments of pause into your routine to cultivate mindfulness and enhance your overall well-being.*

---

* To access this exercise/meditation online, please visit www.christincollins.com.

"In the attitude of silence, the soul finds the path in a clearer light, and what is elusive and deceptive resolves itself into crystal clearness."
— MAHATMA GANDHI

let go

_____

_"In the process of letting go, you will lose many things
from the past, but you will find yourself."_
— DEEPAK CHOPRA

Judging others, judging ourselves—how do we break free from the grip
of pain, betrayal, trauma, and loss? How do we extend forgiveness to
ourselves? How do we let go?

One of the most far-reaching and transformative steps I've learned
on my healing journey is to welcome the art of letting go. Letting
go is not an act of defeat but rather a courageous choice to untangle
ourselves from the knots of the past and open ourselves to the boundless
possibilities of the present moment.

At the heart of letting go lies the recognition of our attachment to
judgment—the bonds that tether us to people, experiences, outcomes,
and that longing for control. Through self-inquiry and reflection,
I've been working on uncovering the subtle ways attachment has
manifested in my life and how it has shaped my perceptions, behaviors,

and relationships. My investigations brought me to Glennon Doyle's transformative book, *Untamed.* Within these pages, I truly began to thrive and experience an unprecedented breakthrough.

This passage, in particular, resonated with me deeply: *"The Truth is that it matters not at all what you think of my life – but it matters supremely what you think of your own. Judgment is just another cage we live in so we don't have to feel, know, and imagine. Judgment is self-abandonment. You are not here to waste your time deciding whether my life is true and beautiful enough for you. You are here to decide if your life, relationships, and world are true and beautiful enough for you. And if they are not, and you dare to admit they are not, you must decide if you have the guts, the right – perhaps the duty – to burn to the ground that which is not true and beautiful enough and get started building what is."*[11]

This awareness continues to transform me. It challenges me to confront my authenticity and question the facades I've built. Am I courageous enough to dismantle what doesn't align with my truth? Am I ready to embody my genuine self without seeking validation or fearing judgment from others?

With my inquisitive nature rooted in research, I sought answers to these questions and a deeper understanding of how science approaches the transformative process of letting go. This curiosity led me to probe into the concept of neuroplasticity and the brain's remarkable capacity to reorganize and adapt in the face of new experiences.

Neuroplasticity refers to the brain's remarkable ability to reorganize itself by forming new neural connections throughout life. It involves the brain's capacity to adapt and change in response to various experiences, environmental influences, learning, and injury. This phenomenon allows the brain to rewire its structure and function, enabling individuals to learn new skills, recover from injuries, and adapt to changes in their environment.[12]

Throughout my career, I've learned from colleagues how neuroplasticity plays a significant role in the process of letting go and in forgiveness. It's been shown that if we hold onto our negative emotions, resentments, or past traumas, whether conscious or unconscious, that our neural pathways associated with these experiences become deeply ingrained in our brain circuitry. Over time, these patterns can reinforce themselves, leading to rumination, anxiety, and an inability to move forward.

Dr. Andrew Huberman, a popular neuroscientist known for his research on brain plasticity, vision, and neural regeneration, has said on his YouTube video, *The Science of Letting Go*, that *"The reflexive thoughts and action patterns that we seem stuck with is its own form of what we call neuroplasticity. It's the brain and nervous systems capacity to change our response to an experience... It's the unlearning, or undoing of that knot (that's been) built into our nervous systems that we can't seem to relieve without doing some deliberate work... The other side of that coin is to replace those behaviors by adding new behaviors or thought patterns."*[13]

As researchers like Dr. Huberman dig into the workings of our neurons, it becomes clear that neuroplasticity offers hope for letting go of unproductive thoughts or patterns by suggesting these patterns are not fixed or immutable. Science demonstrates that we can actively reshape our brain's neural networks through intentional practices, such as mindfulness, cognitive reframing, and forgiveness exercises. By repeatedly engaging in these activities, we can weaken the neural connections associated with negative emotions and strengthen those related to positive emotions, resilience, and compassion.

Forgiveness, in particular, can lead to significant changes in brain structure and function. When we forgive, we activate regions of the brain associated with empathy, understanding, and emotional regulation while dampening activity in areas linked to anger and resentment. This process promotes healing and emotional well-being and cultivates neural flexibility, allowing us greater ease in letting go of past hurts and in moving forward.

The scientific notion that my emotional state could significantly impact my health was initially brought to my attention by Kevin, a friend of my brother-in-law who was a physician's assistant at the time specializing in lifestyle and performance medicine. I had reached out to him to speak at an event I was organizing centered around the role of nutrition and a deeper exploration of trauma's effects on health. During this conversation, I took the opportunity to share some of my health concerns and history with him.

Kevin intently listened to all the details. When I finished telling my story, he didn't hesitate to respond, diagnosing, "Oh, you've blown out your digestive system from being in a chronic state of fight or flight due to your past trauma. Your sympathetic nervous system has been in overdrive, and your body is paying the price. You need to rewire your brain!" Suddenly, the puzzle pieces were sliding into place. How could he land on that so quickly and easily after I had lived with this mystery for decades?

For too long I was saddled with the weight of guilt, shame, and self-disappointment from my past trauma. I unknowingly evaded the present moment, fearing the solitude of introspection would ultimately reveal the truth behind my issues. That cycle eroded my well-being, but not anymore. Today, I cherish my authenticity and love myself unconditionally, accepting my uniqueness. I've experienced the power of forgiveness and the freedom it brings through letting go of self-judgment and blaming others.

I encourage you to get comfortable with loving your vulnerability. Change what no longer feels right. From this place of wholeness and self-love, you can step out into your community and interconnect with others in a positive and healing way. When you show up whole, you can contribute your fullest potential to everything and everyone around you!

At its core, letting go is an act of embracing the flow of life—an acknowledgment that change is inevitable and surrendering to the rhythm of existence is a wisdom that allows life to unfold organically. In embracing the flow of life, we discover a sense of freedom and aliveness that transcends the limitations of attachment.

It's possible to rewrite our stories, starting with love for ourselves and our neurons!

LETTING GO EXERCISE

This meditation exercise helps you cultivate the skill of letting go by releasing attachments to thoughts, emotions, and past experiences.

1. **Set up for Serenity:** Find a comfortable and quiet space where you won't be disturbed for the duration of the meditation. Sit or lie down in a relaxed position, ensuring your spine is straight but not rigid. Close your eyes gently.

2. **Deep Breathing:** Take a few deep breaths, inhaling slowly through your nose and exhaling through your mouth. With each breath, allow yourself to relax deeper into the present moment.

3. **Body Scan and Relaxation:** Shift your awareness to your body. Notice any areas of tension or discomfort and consciously relax those muscles.

4. **Confronting Attachments:** Bring to mind a specific thought, emotion, or experience you've been holding onto and struggling to let go of. It could be a grudge, regret, fear, or any other form of attachment.

5. **Observing without Judgment:** As you hold this thought or feeling in your mind, observe it without judgment. Notice how it feels in your body and the thoughts that arise.

6. **Symbolic Release:** Now, imagine yourself holding onto this thought or feeling in the palm of your hand. Visualize it as an object—a feather, a cloud, or any other symbol that resonates with you.

7. **Letting Go Visualization:** Take a deep breath in and imagine releasing this object from your hand as you exhale. Watch it float away from you, carried by a gentle breeze or drifting into the distance.

8. **Affirming Freedom:** As you breathe deeply, repeat a mantra or affirmation to yourself, such as "I release what no longer serves me" or "I am free from attachment."

9. **Embracing Lightness:** Allow yourself to sit in this space of release and surrender for a few moments, basking in the lightness and freedom that comes with letting go—basking in love. You are love!

10. **Express Gratitude:** Take a moment to express gratitude for the experience of letting go and the opportunity for growth it has provided you. Reflect on the lessons learned and your newfound sense of freedom you have cultivated. Offer thanks to yourself for your willingness to engage in this practice of release and self-discovery.

11. **Return to Reality:** When you feel ready, slowly bring your awareness back to your surroundings. Wiggle your fingers and toes, gently stretch your body, and open your eyes.

12. **Reflection:** Take a moment to reflect on your experience and any insights that arose during the meditation. Acknowledge the courage to let go and the empowerment from releasing attachments.*

---

* To access this exercise/meditation online, please visit www.christincollins.com.

"Love is the absence of judgment."

— DALAI LAMA

open heart

"The most valuable possession you can own is an open heart."
— CARLOS SANTANA

The heart serves as both a compass and a sanctuary, guiding us through the ebbs and flows of life's path. At its core lies a meaningful capacity for openness—a willingness to accept the richness of existence with vulnerability and courage.

Keeping an open heart is more than a passive state of being; it's a conscious choice and a commitment to engage with the world with empathy, compassion, and authenticity. Cultivating an open heart cannot be underestimated in an era marked by division and uncertainty. It is the key to fostering connection, healing wounds, and transcending barriers of fear and misunderstanding.

As I reflect on my challenges in learning to open my heart, I find it ironic that my struggle wasn't so much with giving love but instead with receiving it. How could I allow real, deep, inspiring love into my heart? After all, what would happen when someone leaves? When they disappoint me? When they hurt me? Notice how I said *when* and not even *if.* That's just how I saw life.

Because of that, it felt safer and easier to love from a distance and express love in only one direction—out. I could love the heck out of you, but there was no way I could receive the same in return. Deflecting love shielded me from being caught off guard and experiencing heartbreak. Or so I subconsciously believed.

My reluctance to receive has extended to other forms of support, such as kindness, generosity, and assistance. While I excel at giving from the depths of my heart, I have built walls to prevent myself from accepting these gifts in return. I became aware of this pattern more than two decades ago and still struggle with it today.

My first glimpse into this issue came in 2000 when I met my strikingly handsome husband-to-be on a blind date. Oddly, it wasn't *his* love that I kept at bay. Having been through a divorce before, I knew I could survive if things didn't work out. With that life experience, I found the courage to open my heart to David without any strings attached. The real challenge arose, however, in opening my heart to his two beautiful children. Now, that could destroy me!

I met Brendan and Meghan when they were seven and five years old. On our first Christmas together, I poured my heart into creating a magical day for us. I meticulously planned decorations, meals, and gifts, eager to make everything perfect. Christmas morning found me in David's holiday-infused living room, holding an aromatic cup of coffee in my festive mug, camera at hand, ready to witness the culmination of all my hard work. The presents were exquisitely wrapped, color-coordinated for each recipient, and perfectly placed under our Hallmark-worthy Christmas tree. What a joy for me to spend this special day with these incredible people.

All was going swimmingly well as the kids took turns unwrapping each gift with appreciation and gratitude. They squealed, jumped up and down, ran over to give hugs, and eagerly dove into enjoying their new treasures. Even more heartwarming was David's loving gaze directed at me, grateful for all that I had done to make this Christmas morning so merry and bright. Yep, life was amazing.

Suddenly, it was my turn to receive. Little Brendan, with his bowl haircut and beaming smile, shyly approached me. With arms extended, he held out a small, preciously wrapped package as only a seven-year-old could. His mixture of shyness and excitement to share created such an authentic moment in time. Brendan's young life had been full of twists and turns as he navigated his parents' divorce, now dividing his time between two separate homes. I admired Brendan's determination and thoughtfulness to take a chance on me as he stood before me with his gift.

As a token of our relationship, the vulnerability of this gift literally knocked the wind out of me. Brendan's willingness to show me love, to include me in his holiday thoughts, and to wrap the darn present himself touched me deeply. I couldn't breathe. Fumbling like a complete fool, I barely whispered "thank you" as he wished me a Merry Christmas and placed his gift in my hands. Awkwardly, I put it aside, eager to turn our attention away to someone or something else—anything to escape this moment so I could recompose myself and feel secure behind the steel wall around my heart.

Thankfully, his little sister, Meghan, came to my rescue, galloping over with a present of her own to share with me. Excitedly, she jumped up and down, exclaiming, "Open it, open it!" I laughed, almost spilling my coffee everywhere. She had broken the spell, and I successfully tucked my heart into safe hiding. I opened both presents with a smooth, adulting calm, and exclaimed how much they meant to me.

Later that evening, as the magical day was coming to a close, David thanked me for the wonderful day we had. With love, he then offered some unexpected but insightful feedback. He asked me how I felt watching the kids open the gifts I had chosen for them. I gushed, thinking about the joy it had brought to me. Then, he questioned why I struggled to receive in return, which really struck a chord.

David explained that by holding back from accepting love from others, I denied *them* the joy of giving. That revelation has stayed with me, and as I mentioned, I still work on being open to receiving. It's been perhaps one of my biggest lessons to fully understand; true loving requires both giving and receiving love.

An open heart involves vulnerability and authenticity, allowing ourselves to be seen and felt fully by others. When we embrace vulnerability and authenticity, we create space for love to flow freely in both directions, as love thrives in an environment of openness and honesty.

Over the subsequent years, I have explored this profound revelation further. A few brave souls in science and medicine showcase the necessity of dropping into the heart and connecting with oneness from a place of wholeness for bettering our health, well-being, and quality of life. I've had the privilege of listening to the wisdom of Dr. Daniel Siegel, a maverick leader in the field.

I became intrigued by Dr. Siegel's work during his presentation at a mindfulness conference I attended. In his groundbreaking book, *Aware*, he offers an alternative lens for viewing ourselves and the importance of connecting with our heart, and the positive effects that has for our brain.

He writes, *"Scientists in the past rarely wrote about love, so naturally I feel the echoes of that professional discomfort in speaking directly about this essential aspect of our lives. Trained as an attachment researcher, though, I know that the health of our lives depends on the love in our relationships. And as a scientist familiar with the brain, I know, too, that love in a relationship supports the optimal growth of the brain's integration, enabling it to function in a coordinated and balanced way as widely separated regions become linked to one another."*[14]

Dr. Siegel's insights underscore the profound interplay between our emotional connections and brain function, highlighting the imperativeness of nurturing love and compassion within ourselves and our relationships for a harmonious and integrated life.

Further to the significance of maintaining an open heart, I acknowledge the contributions of many colleagues at the forefront of HeartMath®. This science-based system explores the intricate connection between our hearts and overall well-being.

At its core, the HeartMath® Institute emphasizes the importance of coherence, a state where the heart, mind, and emotions are in harmony. This coherence is a physiological phenomenon deeply intertwined with our emotional and psychological states. It allows us to connect with ourselves and others on a deeper level, fostering understanding and harmony in our relationships.

The heart-focused breathing approach of HeartMath® cultivates positive emotions like gratitude and appreciation, which, together, can help facilitate this openness. By practicing these techniques, we learn to regulate our emotions, reduce stress, and increase our resilience to life's challenges.

Moreover, HeartMath® research shows that consciously shifting our focus to positive emotions and coherent heart rhythms improves our physiological state. Our heart rate variability becomes more balanced, which indicates a state of coherence that promotes overall well-being.[15]

Living from the heart is authentic living. We must open our hearts and maintain that openness through every experience, good or bad. We choose how we perceive life; it is synonymous with embodying love, which entails embracing vulnerability, fostering connection, practicing acceptance, expressing generosity, and cultivating gratitude. These fundamental aspects of love offer us deeper fulfillment and joy.

HEART-OPENING EXERCISE

This exercise helps you cultivate openness and compassion by practicing a heart-opening meditation.

1. **Prepare Your Space:** Find a quiet and comfortable space to sit or lie down without distractions. Close your eyes gently, and take a few deep breaths to center yourself.

2. **Connect with Your Heart Center:** Begin by placing your hands over your heart center, feeling the warmth and energy radiating from this area. Take a moment to connect with your heart space, allowing yourself to become fully present in the moment.

3. **Illuminate Your Heart Space:** Visualize a soft, warm light emanating from your heart, expanding with each breath you take. Imagine this light growing brighter and more expansive with every inhale, filling your chest.

4. **Summon Love and Joy:** As you breathe deeply, bring to mind someone or something that brings you feelings of love, gratitude, or joy. It could be a loved one, a pet, a cherished memory, or simply something in nature that resonates with you.

5. **Immerse in Loving Emotions:** Hold this image in your mind and allow yourself to fully experience the emotions associated with it. Notice how your heart space feels as you connect with these feelings of love and appreciation.

6. **Extend Love to Yourself:** Now, gently shift your focus to yourself. Visualize sending the same feelings of love, compassion, and acceptance toward yourself. Offer yourself kindness and forgiveness, acknowledging your inherent worthiness. Surround yourself with love. You are love!

7. **Inhale Love, Exhale Compassion:** As you breathe in, imagine inhaling love and compassion into your heart space. As you exhale, imagine sending this love out into the world, sharing it with others around you.

8. **Sustain Your Heart's Radiance:** Continue this practice for several minutes, allowing yourself to bask in the warmth and openness of your heart. If your mind starts to wander, gently guide your focus to your breath and the sensations in your heart space.

9. **Affirm Your Love and Gratitude:** Repeat a loving-kindness affirmation or mantra silently or aloud to reinforce your feelings of love and gratitude. For example, "I am filled with love and gratitude" or "I am thankful for the abundance of blessings in my life."

10. **Conclude with Mindful Reflection:** When you feel ready, slowly release your hands from your heart center and take a few more deep breaths. Wiggle your fingers and toes, gradually bringing your awareness to the present moment.

11. **Integrate and Apply:** Take a moment to reflect on your experience. Notice any shifts in your mood, energy, or outlook after practicing this heart-opening meditation. Consider integrating this practice into your daily routine to cultivate greater openness and compassion.*

---

* To access this exercise/meditation online, please visit www.christincollins.com.

"The only lasting beauty is the beauty of the heart."

— RUMI

visualize

---

*"Create the highest grandest vision possible for your life,
because you become what you believe."*

— OPRAH WINFREY

I'm thrilled at this point to embark on exploring visualization and its
weighty impact on human potential. My journey with visualization
began with the wise words of Heather Christie, a nationally celebrated
thought leader, public speaker, executive coach, and dear friend, who
instilled in me the principle of *casting my vision unattached to outcome*
several years ago. Since then, I've valued this philosophy as my
guiding principle. Whenever I pursue a goal, I commit wholeheartedly,
regardless of the eventual outcome, choosing to savor every moment.
Time and again, I've been amazed by the results—whether my original
goal materialized or the path took an unexpected turn, leading to even
greater outcomes.

Visualization, also known as the process of creating mental images,
became significant in my life during the mundane routine of my
previous career in healthcare. I approached health and well-being

from a different perspective than the system because I was passionate about the mind-body connection. My focus was on preventing disease rather than treating it after the fact, which left me out of sync with the healthcare culture. I was steadfast about my ideals because I was living proof of its efficacy.

As I plodded on through the years, I felt stifled and silenced as my vibrant ideas were met with indifference or disdain. Gradually, I lost confidence in my abilities and sank into a pit of self-doubt and resignation. Each workday became a dreaded chore, a repetitive cycle of collecting paychecks without experiencing any sense of fulfillment.

Then, during the turmoil of the pandemic, an unexpected opportunity emerged: an early exit package offered by my employer, who was contending with financial strain. It was a chance for liberation, a lifeline in the form of a severance package. Clutching the information packet, I hesitantly broached the topic with my husband, David. As we pored over the details together, the uncertainty was nerve-wracking. What would I do next? How would I replace the stability of my income?

Drawing courage from my practice of *casting my vision unattached to outcome*, I took a deep breath as we decided to take a chance. I accepted the buyout offer without a clear roadmap ahead. It was a leap of faith, a bold step into the unknown. With no safety net to cushion my fall, I seized the uncertainty, fueled by fear and exhilaration.

Transitioning into entrepreneurship, I faced the challenges of forging my new path. The experience was filled with obstacles and moments of self-doubt, often threatening to derail my progress. However, in those moments, I turned to visualization as a tool for clarity and direction. I envisioned my desired future, painting vivid mental pictures of success and fulfillment. Through practicing visualization, I cultivated a sense of purpose and direction, aligning my actions with my deepest desires.

With each visualization session, I tapped into the limitless potential of my imagination, exploring new possibilities and charting a course toward my goals. Visualization became my North Star, guiding me with clarity and confidence. I began to see tangible results as opportunities emerged seemingly out of thin air, aligning with the visions I had cultivated in my mind's eye. With each small success, my confidence grew, fueling my determination to press onward.

Visualization has become more than just a tool for success for me; it has become a way of life. I have learned to trust in the power of my imagination, harnessing its creative energy to shape my reality. Through visualization, I unlock the door to my true potential, stepping into a future filled with possibility and purpose.

Of course, beyond my evidence-based experiences, I've investigated the scientific underpinnings of visualization, bringing me back to the mechanisms of neuroplasticity. I have learned from colleagues that when we visualize, we engage in mental rehearsals that activate specific neural pathways, mirroring the effects of actual experiences. Neuroimaging studies have revealed how vividly visualizing tasks activates corresponding brain regions, blurring the lines between imagination and reality.

This makes mental rehearsal—or visualization—a scientifically valuable tool for optimizing performance in many ways. Stories of personal triumph and collective inspiration bridge the gap between intention and realization. Whether it's athletes visualizing victory or activists envisioning social change, visualization can be the catalyst for intense shifts in individuals and society. Through visualization, we can all tap into our inner creativity and engage in a process of self-discovery and empowerment.

I've read a fantastic book titled *Into the Magic Shop* by Dr. James R. Doty. What moved me was Dr. Doty's transition from being a neurosurgeon—a left-brain doctor—to learning the art of manifesting from the heart. While pursuing dreams through the conscious ego is common, creating with heart coherence, as he suggests, takes it to the next level. One of my favorite passages from the book is as follows.

"When our brain changes, we change. That is a truth proven by science. But an even greater truth is that when our heart changes, everything changes. And that change is not only in how we see the world but in how the world sees us. And in how the world responds to us."[16]

From this statement, I've learned the importance of visualizing from both my mind and heart—an *open heart,* to be more precise!

Connecting to the heart and leading a life from that space is soul-transforming. Getting to this point may be challenging for many of us; I know it sure has been for me over the years. When I first started to manifest from my heart, it hurt. I mean really, truly hurt, to the point where I thought I was having a heart attack. I sat with the pain and embraced it, thanked it for visiting, and gave honor to all the hurt and betrayal it has endured: shame, guilt, self-loathing—you name it. But it gets much easier as my practice unfolds, and the results have been life-altering.

There is a final important note about manifestation to mention here, which brings me back to Heather Christie's original advice to *cast my vision unattached to outcome* and also to Dr. Joe Dispenza's work, whose unique genius blends science, spirituality, and the human experience with divine ease and grace.

In his book, *Breaking the Habit of Being Yourself,* Dr. Dispenza shares, *"We do not have to do anything other than visualize what we want from our open hearts, connect with the feeling of that experience, and then let that permeate out like a blinking transmitter. The rest is up to the collective energy."*[17]

So, hold a clear intention of what you want but leave the "how" details to the unpredictable quantum field. Let it orchestrate an event in your life in a way that is just right for you. If you're going to expect anything, expect the unexpected. Surrender, trust, and let go of how a desired event will unfold.

As I continue my journey—*yes, this is a lifelong process*—I continue to learn the importance of consistency, intentionality, and self-awareness in sustaining a visualization practice. Integrating gratitude, surrender, and adaptability into my approach, I have cultivated a fertile ground where my dreams flourish. I visualize my highest self, then show up as that person.

Reflecting on my progress, I realize visualization has opened doors to endless possibilities for me when guided by my inner vision. Through the power of imagination, I continually discover the extraordinary within, unshackling my heart and transforming me again, blossoming into a beautiful lotus flower, butterfly, or dragonfly.

HEART-CENTERED VISUALIZATION EXERCISE

1. **Set the Stage:** Find a quiet and comfortable space to sit or lie down without distractions. Take a few deep breaths to center yourself and let go of any tension or stress.

2. **Connect with Your Heart:** Place your hand over your heart and take a moment to connect with the energy center in your chest. Feel the warmth and rhythm of your heartbeat as you focus on this area.

3. **Cultivate Gratitude:** Close your eyes and bring to mind something or someone you are deeply grateful for. It could be a person, a pet, a place, or a moment in your life. Fully immerse yourself in gratitude, filling your heart with warmth and appreciation.

4. **Set Your Intention:** Consider what you would like to visualize or manifest in your life. It could be a specific goal, a desired outcome, or simply a feeling you wish to cultivate. Positively frame your intention with empowering affirmations such as "I am" or "I have."

5. **Visualize with Love:** With your intention, visualize the desired outcome as if it has already happened. See it clearly in your mind's eye, using all your senses to create a vivid and detailed image. Imagine yourself immersed in this reality, feeling the joy, love, and fulfillment it brings.

6. **Engage Your Heart:** As you visualize, focus on the feelings of love and compassion emanating from your heart. Imagine these feelings radiating outward, infusing your visualization with positive energy and magnetizing it toward you.

7. **Embrace Gratitude Again:** Before concluding your visualization, take another moment to express gratitude for the manifestation of your intention. Thank the universe, or whatever higher power you believe in, for bringing this reality into your life.

8. **Ground Yourself:** Slowly bring your awareness to the present moment. Wiggle your fingers and toes, take a few deep breaths, and gently open your eyes. Take note of how you feel after completing the exercise.

9. **Reflect and Journal:** Take some time to reflect on your visualization experience. Journal about any insights, feelings, or sensations that arose during the exercise. Notice any shifts in your mood, energy, or perspective.

10. **Practice Regularly:** Include visualization from the heart as a regular practice in your daily routine. Each day, set aside time to connect with your heart, cultivate gratitude, and visualize your intentions with love and compassion. Allow yourself to surrender to the process and trust in the power of your heart-centered visualization practice.*

---

* To access this exercise/meditation online, please visit www.christincollins.com.

"The power of imagination makes us infinite."

— JOHN MUIR

energize

"Everything is energy and that's all there is to it.
Match the frequency of the reality you
want and you cannot help but get
that reality. It can be no other way.
This is not philosophy. This is physics."
— ALBERT EINSTEIN

What is energy?

Albert Einstein's theory of relativity, particularly his famous equation $E=mc^2$, revolutionized our understanding of energy. In this equation:

- E represents energy
- m represents mass
- c represents the speed of light in a vacuum

Einstein's equation shows that energy and mass are interchangeable; they are different forms of the same thing, which means that mass can be converted into energy and vice versa.

Understanding this concept of energy and its connection to everything has been a leap for me, but once I started to digest it, it became elegantly simple and made total sense. Dr. Bruce Lipton's work in his book *The Biology of Belief* describes how *"Einstein revealed that we do not live in a universe with discrete, physical objects separated by dead space. The Universe is one indivisible, dynamic whole in which energy and matter are so deeply entangled it is impossible to consider them as independent elements."*[18]

If you had told me in high school that I would be attracted to physics, or even write about it someday, I would have laughed loudly. But now, as I simplify these ideas, they're the baseline for me to understand what I already intuitively know. We *are* one. Everything *is* interconnected, and I can, in fact, feel it before I see it.

This realization leads me to think about the concept of entanglement. Even if physics isn't your jam, please stick with me here. In the realm of quantum mechanics, entanglement is a phenomenon where the properties of two or more particles become correlated in such a way that the state of one particle instantaneously influences the state of another, regardless of the distance between them. Albert Einstein famously called this "spooky action at a distance," and it challenges our traditional ideas of cause and effect.

Entanglement is more than a theoretical curiosity; it is experimentally verified with far-reaching implications for our understanding of the nature of our existence and challenging our classical notions of separateness and individuality.[19]

How does this insight manifest in our daily experiences? How does it influence love?

To answer those questions, let's discuss the frequency of love for a moment. Love is often described as a potent energy vibrating at a high frequency. When we embody love, we emit positive energy that harmonizes with the vibrations of others and the world around us—through that theory of quantum entanglement business. I believe this "resonance" can create a ripple effect, uplifting and inspiring those we encounter on an energetic level.

With emotional energy, we often use the terms *low energy* or *high energy*.

Low-energy vibrations typically represent feelings of negativity, fear, sadness, anger, or apathy. When someone or something emits low-energy vibrations, it can drain our energy levels and leave us feeling depleted, stressed, or disheartened. Examples of low-energy vibrations include gossiping, holding onto grudges, or surrounding ourselves with negative influences.

On the other hand, high-energy vibrations signify positivity, joy, love, gratitude, and vitality. When we encounter individuals or experiences emitting high-energy vibrations, we often feel uplifted, inspired, and motivated. These interactions can boost our mood, increase our enthusiasm, and enhance our overall well-being. Examples of high-energy vibrations include acts of kindness, moments of laughter, or spending time in nature.

It's important to be mindful of the energies we surround ourselves with, as they can significantly impact our mental, emotional, and even physical state. Consciously aligning ourselves with high-energy vibrations and minimizing exposure to low-energy ones cultivates a more fulfilling and harmonious life. Similar to removing that root cause thorn we discussed earlier, it can sometimes be easier said than done.

Every human's expression of energy is uniquely shaped by their life experiences, biases, and defaults. Have you ever shared a moment with someone only to hear them express a vastly different viewpoint? How could the same event be perceived so differently? It's a common occurrence for me. I naturally lean toward optimism, seeking the silver lining in any situation. Yet, when others focus on scarcity, it's as jarring as a police siren to my brain. Why do they see negativity while I perceive opportunity, love, and light?

The key lies in the multitude of ways to experience a moment. We have the power to choose our perception by the energy we bring to a situation. Whether we dwell in negativity or embrace the moment's lessons, our energy follows suit, offering a transformative shift. In the words of author James Redfield, *"Where attention goes, energy flows."*

Considering the influence of our experiences, I'm brought back to Dr. Joe Dispenza's book, *Breaking the Habit of Being Yourself.*

"If we have experienced suffering, and within our minds and bodies we hold that suffering and express it through our thoughts and feelings, we broadcast that energetic signature into the field. The universal intelligence responds by sending into our lives another event that will reproduce the same intellectual and emotional response."

He further explains that we need to break our addiction to our more primal survival emotions, because when we can do that, we raise our level of consciousness.[20]

Dr. Dispenza's words tell me that we *can* control our vibration levels. Depression, anger, hate, and jealousy are low-vibrating emotions that keep us attracting other low-vibrating experiences. Want to vibe high?

Spend time connecting with love, kindness, compassion, and joy in your heart.

Life presents us with lessons that offer opportunities for growth, to reconnect with oneness, and to remember that we are all interconnected and that *we are love*. Understanding that we are all energy condensed into matter allows us to view our experiences and surroundings with a new understanding.

Why is this not widely known, shouted from every mountaintop, and prescribed in every doctor's office? Well, that's a whole other book. For now, Dr. Bruce Lipton shares, *"I believe the major reason why energy research has been all but ignored comes down to dollars and cents. The trillion-dollar pharmaceutical industry puts its research money into the search for magic bullets in the form of chemicals because pills mean money. If energy healing could be made into tablet form, drug manufacturers would get interested quickly."*[21]

The energy of love has the innate ability to heal and transform. When we approach life with love, we cultivate an environment of compassion, acceptance, and forgiveness. This energy can dissolve barriers, heal wounds, and bring profound personal growth and healing. Love also acts as a magnet, drawing to us the people, opportunities, and experiences that align with our highest good.

To *be. love.* means to express our true essence authentically and unconditionally. When we allow love to guide our thoughts, words, and actions, we become conduits for pure, authentic energy. This authenticity attracts genuine connections and fosters deep relationships, allowing us to navigate challenges with resilience and grace.

ELEVATING YOUR ENERGY TO THE FREQUENCY OF LOVE EXERCISE

1. **Set Intentions:** Begin by setting your intention to elevate your energy to the frequency of love. Take a moment to reflect on the power of love to transform your inner state and the world around you.

2. **Find a Quiet Space:** Find a quiet and comfortable space to sit or lie down without distractions. Close your eyes gently and take a few deep breaths to center yourself.

3. **Cultivate Gratitude:** Start by cultivating gratitude within your heart. Reflect on the blessings and abundance in your life, big and small. Express gratitude for the love you have received, the experiences that have shaped you, and the beauty of the present moment.

4. **Connect with Your Heart Center:** Place your hand over your heart and connect with the energy center in the middle of your chest. Visualize a warm, glowing light emanating from your heart, expanding with each breath you take.

5. **Invoke Loving Intentions:** With each inhale, imagine breathing in love and compassion. With each exhale, release any tension or negativity stored within your body and mind. Set loving intentions for yourself and others, wishing happiness, peace, and well-being for all.

6. **Practice Self-Love:** Shower yourself with love and kindness. Embrace yourself exactly as you are, recognizing your inherent worthiness and divine essence. Offer words of affirmation and encouragement, nurturing a deep sense of self-love and acceptance.

7. **Extend Love to Others:** Expand the circle of love beyond yourself to encompass your loved ones, friends, acquaintances, and even strangers. Visualize sending energetic waves of love and compassion to all beings, wishing them joy, healing, and fulfillment.

8. **Cultivate Compassion:** Cultivate compassion by empathizing with the joys and sorrows of others. Imagine yourself stepping into their shoes, feeling their emotions with an open and empathetic heart. Send loving-kindness to those who are suffering, offering them comfort and support.

9. **Radiate Love into the World:** Allow the love within your heart to radiate outward, permeating the world with its healing energy. Visualize your love merging with the collective consciousness, uplifting and inspiring all beings to awaken to the power of love.

10. **Express Gratitude:** Take a moment to express gratitude for this practice and the transformative power of love. Acknowledge the shifts you have experienced in your energy and outlook, knowing that love has the power to create profound change within and without.

11. **Open Your Eyes:** When you feel ready, gently open your eyes and be present. Carry the energy of love with you throughout your day, throughout your life, embodying compassion, kindness, and joy in all your interactions.

You now know how to—*be. love.**

---

* To access this exercise/meditation online, please visit www.christincollins.com.

"Change your energy, change your life."

— DR. JOE DISPENZA

---

prioritize

---

*"The key is not to prioritize what's on your schedule,
but to schedule your priorities."*
— STEPHEN COVEY

Are you eager to use your newfound skills to *be. love.*?

I know I certainly am! I also know that for many of us, putting ourselves first can be the biggest challenge we will face on that journey.

In today's society, many of us find ourselves caught in a relentless pursuit of health, happiness, and wealth, often at an unsustainable pace. We've come a long way from our survival days, living in caves and being chased by saber-toothed tigers. But why do so many of us still tax our minds, bodies, and adrenal glands in a constant fight-or-flight mode despite knowing how detrimental it is to us? Why can't we prioritize ourselves amidst the societal pressures and distractions of our lives?

I'd like to suggest that it's time to awaken to the truth; our health and happiness lie within us, not outside of us. It's time to prioritize

prioritize · 127

ourselves, recognize our intrinsic value, and nurture our well-being as we evolve as human *beings*. When we prioritize self-love, we cultivate a deep sense of connection with ourselves, fostering resilience, confidence, and inner peace.

Conversely, neglecting self-love can lead to a myriad of challenges, including burnout, low self-esteem, and mental health issues. When we fail to prioritize our well-being, we may find ourselves trapped in cycles of self-criticism, comparison, and people-pleasing, diminishing our capacity for joy and fulfillment.

Prioritizing self-love extends far beyond individual benefits. Now that we understand how energy works, we can see that it reverberates throughout our relationships, work, and communities. When we cultivate a deep reservoir of self-love, we become more compassionate, empathetic, and authentic in our interactions with others. Our capacity to give and receive love expands to everything and everyone around us.

It may seem easy to say, "Just put yourself at the top of your to-do list, and the rest will fall into place," but I think most of us know how challenging that can be. So, for me, sometimes it's just about taking baby steps to slowly integrate practices in my life until I finally feel the scales tip in my favor.

That might simply involve going to bed earlier so that I can wake up earlier for a meditative walk before starting my day. Other times, it might require a bigger life adjustment, like leaving a respectable career to follow my true purpose. It's been quite an experience as I continually learn, grow, and adapt to find more balance in my world.

With that in mind, rather than providing an exercise for this chapter, I'd like to share my *top ten list of life priorities* that have been instrumental in my journey toward self-love. Please feel free to use this entire list or select components to help you formulate your personalized list of self-love priorities.

Again, these are practices that we can all do for free. When we prioritize our well-being, it ripples out to positively affect everything around us!

MY TOP TEN LIST OF LIFE PRIORITIES

1. **Prioritize Sleep:** Quality sleep is essential for physical health, mental clarity, and emotional well-being. It allows the body to rest, repair, and recharge, promoting overall vitality.

For years, I struggled with sleep issues, often sacrificing rest to meet deadlines or catch up on tasks. I viewed sleep as a luxury rather than a necessity, believing I could function just fine on minimal rest. However, I soon realized the significant impact sleep deprivation was having on my overall well-being.

During this time, I experienced frequent bouts of fatigue, irritability, and difficulty concentrating. Simple tasks felt overwhelming, and my productivity suffered as a result. I also noticed changes in my mood and emotional stability, often feeling more anxious and stressed than usual.

It wasn't until I made a conscious effort to prioritize quality sleep that I began to see significant improvements in my physical, mental, and emotional health. I enhanced deep and restorative sleep by establishing a consistent bedtime routine and creating a sleep-friendly environment.

Prioritizing quality sleep transformed my life because, with improved rest, I feel more energized, focused, and emotionally balanced during the day. I can now confidently say that consistent quality sleep is essential for well-being.

2. **Make Movement a Habit and Get Grounded:** Regular physical activity is crucial for maintaining optimal health and vitality. It strengthens muscles, improves cardiovascular health, enhances mood, and boosts energy levels.

Movement has been an integral part of my daily routine for as long as I can remember. I've always valued the invigorating effects of physical activity on my body and mind, whether it's a brisk walk or a triathlon. Most people understand the value of being active. Gentle routine movement is a cornerstone of the influential research done by the Blue Zones Project, a study that has examined the habits of places around the world where people often live to be one hundred years old.

Another aspect of my movement routine that I've come to appreciate deeply is the practice of grounding with the earth, perhaps something that's not as well understood. Spending time outdoors, particularly barefoot, allows me to connect with nature on an intimate level and reap the benefits of what's known as *earthing* or *grounding*.

During walks in a park or strolls along a beach, I routinely make a conscious effort to kick off my shoes and feel the earth beneath my feet. This simple grounding provides a sensory experience and has incredible health benefits.

Studies have shown that direct contact with the earth's surface can have a therapeutic effect on the body, thanks to the transfer of electrons between our bodies and the earth. This process has been linked to reduced inflammation, improved sleep, and enhanced overall well-being.

Personally, I've noticed that grounding with the earth leaves me feeling refreshed, rejuvenated, and more centered. It's as if the earth's energy grounds me in the present moment, washing away any tension or stress I may be carrying.

3. **Cultivate a Positive Attitude:** Maintaining a positive mindset can significantly impact your overall well-being. It helps reduce stress, increase resilience, and improve your ability to overcome challenges— bringing us back to our discussions on energy and neuroplasticity.

When we cultivate a positive mindset, we influence our well-being and the energy we emit into the world around us. Positive thoughts and emotions ripple, affecting the people and circumstances we encounter. By radiating positivity, we attract similar energy back into our lives, creating a cycle of abundance and joy.

This phenomenon is often described as *the law of attraction*, where like attracts like. When we focus on positive thoughts and intentions, we align ourselves with opportunities and experiences that resonate with our desires and aspirations.

Moreover, the concept of neuroplasticity underscores the remarkable adaptability of the human brain. By consistently engaging in positive thinking patterns, we can literally rewire our brains to perceive the world in a more optimistic light. As we train our minds to focus on the good in every situation, our neural pathways strengthen, making positivity our default mode of operation. Over time, this rewiring leads to a wonderful shift in our outlook on life, enabling us to navigate challenges with grace and optimism.

4. **Eat Wisely:** Nourishing your body with nutritious foods is key to overall health and vitality. Focus on consuming a balanced diet of fruits, vegetables, lean proteins, and whole grains to fuel your body and mind.

My process of prioritizing wise food choices began when I decided to transition to a primarily vegan diet for health and ethical reasons. Initially, I didn't fully grasp the impact that food could have on my well-being. However, as I embarked on this new dietary path, I became increasingly aware of the powerful connection between what I ate and how I felt.

Transitioning to a plant-based diet opened my eyes to a world of vibrant fruits, vegetables, legumes, and whole grains. As I incorporated these nutrient-rich foods into my meals, I noticed substantial changes in my energy levels, mental clarity, and overall sense of vitality. I no longer viewed food as mere sustenance but as a source of nourishment and healing for my body and mind.

Choosing plant-based foods became an act of self-love, a way of honoring my body and prioritizing my health above all else. Over time, my path toward wise eating has developed into a deeply ingrained lifestyle, guided by the belief that what we consume directly impacts our health and vitality. The adage "you are what you eat" may be cliché, but it holds true. By embracing a plant-based diet, I've transformed my relationship with food and cultivated a greater sense of well-being and harmony with both myself and the planet.

5. **Connect with Others:** Building and nurturing meaningful relationships with family, friends, and a supportive community is essential for emotional health and well-being. It provides a sense of belonging and fulfillment.

Highlighting the pivotal role of social connections in promoting overall well-being, the Blue Zones Project has these longevity "Blue Zone" hotspots where individuals maintain close-knit networks characterized by strong familial bonds, deep friendships, faith-based practices, and a sense of belonging to a larger community.

Drawing inspiration from the Blue Zones findings, I recognize the far-reaching impact of meaningful relationships on my emotional health and well-being. Sharing laughter with family members, engaging in heartfelt conversations with close friends, and participating in community events all foster connections with others, enriching my life in countless ways.

6. **Practice Self-Care:** Prioritizing self-care activities, such as relaxation, meditation, or hobbies, is vital for maintaining balance and reducing stress.

Relaxation is a fundamental practice for me. It allows me to unwind, recharge, and restore my energy reserves. Whether through deep-breathing exercises, progressive muscle relaxation, or indulging in a soothing bath, carving out time for relaxation helps alleviate stress and promotes a sense of calm and inner peace.

Meditation is another powerful self-care practice that I've emphasized throughout these *be. love.* pages. By dedicating time to quiet my mind, cultivate mindfulness, and connect with my inner self, meditation is a potent tool for reducing anxiety, enhancing clarity, and fostering emotional resilience. Meditation is like tending to a garden—spending a whole day in the garden before a big event won't make it flourish. Similarly, meditation isn't a quick fix for crises; it's a consistent practice that gradually enriches your everyday life.

In addition to relaxation and meditation, I've found that engaging in hobbies and leisure activities that bring me joy and fulfillment are essential for practicing self-care. Whether pursuing creative outlets like writing, building a puzzle, or simply enjoying quiet moments of solitude reading a good book, incorporating activities that nourish my passions and interests enriches my life and nurtures my well-being.

Throughout *this* book, I've offered a variety of exercises and practices designed to cultivate self-care and promote holistic well-being. From guided meditations and journaling prompts to mindfulness exercises and gratitude practices, I intend each activity to support us in prioritizing self-care and nurturing our overall health and happiness.

By incorporating these self-care practices into our daily routine, we can cultivate a greater sense of balance, resilience, and inner peace, allowing us to navigate life's challenges with grace and authenticity. Remember that prioritizing self-care is not selfish; it's an essential act of self-love that enables us to show up fully for ourselves and others, leading to a more fulfilling and meaningful life.

7. **Set Boundaries:** Establishing healthy boundaries in all areas of your life helps protect your time, energy, and emotional well-being. It allows you to focus on what truly matters and avoid burnout.

Realizing that prioritizing myself also involves acknowledging and honoring my needs without guilt or hesitation has significantly shifted my personal growth. It means setting clear boundaries and learning to say *no* to commitments or situations that detract from my well-being or don't align with my values.

By doing so, I've created space in my life for activities and relationships that genuinely bring me joy, fulfillment, and a sense of purpose. It's about understanding that my time and energy are precious resources. I must invest them wisely in things that nourish my soul and contribute positively to my overall well-being.

8. **Pursue Personal Growth:** Continuously seek opportunities for learning, growth, and self-improvement through setting goals, challenging yourself, and stepping outside your comfort zone to reach your full potential.

The five decades leading me to this moment in time have been an incredible path of self-discovery. Each experience, whether joyful or challenging, has contributed to shaping the person I am today. Along the way, I've often been stepping into the unknown, unsure where the path would lead me. Yet, with each leap of faith, I've discovered new facets of myself and unlocked hidden potential.

Embracing personal growth means constantly pushing beyond our comfort zones and embracing the unfamiliar. It's about venturing into uncharted territory, whether exploring new places, acquiring new skills, or challenging long-held beliefs. For me, this journey has been a continuous process of expansion and evolution, where each new experience serves as an opportunity for learning and self-discovery. There is always more to learn and explore.

Stepping outside our comfort zones allows us to break free from limiting beliefs and tap into our infinite potential. As I progress, I'm filled with excitement and anticipation for the discoveries ahead, understanding that each step brings me closer to realizing my best self.

9. **Cultivate Gratitude:** Regularly practicing gratitude can enhance your overall sense of well-being and happiness. Of course, we've talked about the importance of gratitude already, but one can never overstate its importance!

For me, practicing gratitude is not just a fleeting or momentary emotion; it's a way of life—pausing to reflect on the goodness in my day, no matter how small, and expressing heartfelt appreciation for it.

Keeping a gratitude journal, saying a prayer of thanks, or taking a moment to savor the beauty around me— each act of gratitude strengthens my connection to the energy of abundance and attracts more blessings into my life.

As I cultivate gratitude, I align myself with the highest vibrations of love, joy, and abundance, inviting miracles to unfold in every moment.

10. **Find Purpose and Meaning:** Identify and pursue activities, passions, and goals that give your life meaning and purpose. Having a sense of purpose can provide direction, motivation, and fulfillment.

Even with trials and tribulations on my journey so far, my life's purpose has been so much clearer as I've gotten older. It has been about what truly lights up my soul and brings fulfillment to my life.

As I've gone deeply into introspection, confronting long-held beliefs and assumptions about myself and the world around me, I've seen that many of life's challenges have provided me with invaluable growth. And through these insights, I'm uncovering the underlying threads of my true purpose.

I find my greatest fulfillment in helping others and sharing insights and wisdom from my self-discovery. I am filled with gratitude for the twists and turns, the trials and triumphs that have shaped me into the person I am today.

I hope that within these pages, you've discovered the inspiration to pursue your own sense of meaning on your journey toward your ultimate purpose—to *be. love.**

---

* To access this exercise/meditation online, please visit www.christincollins.com.

> *"Self-care is giving the world the best of you, instead of what's left of you."*
>
> — KATIE REED

Embracing the
be. love. Journey

In this final chapter, we culminate our exploration by synthesizing the meaningful insights and transformative practices unfolding throughout our journey together. We have explored the multifaceted dimensions of what it means to *be. love.*, recognizing that it is not merely a destination but a way of being in the world—a sacred union of self-discovery, compassion, and conscious living.

In summary, we have focused on:

b breathe: At the very core of our existence lies the simple yet profound act of breathing. Through the rhythm of our breath, we connect with the present moment, anchoring ourselves in the here and now. Breathing becomes a gateway to inner peace, clarity, and vitality, reminding us of life's inherent beauty and sanctity.

e emotions: Our emotions serve as messengers, guiding us toward greater self-awareness and authenticity. By embracing the full spectrum of our emotions—joy, sorrow, fear, and love—we honor the richness of our human experience and cultivate emotional resilience and intelligence.

. pause: Amid life's whirlwind, the power of the pause beckons us to slow down, to listen deeply, and to attune to the whispers of our soul. Through intentional pauses, we create space for reflection, discernment, and conscious choice, reclaiming sovereignty over our lives and actions.

l let go: Release becomes a sacred act of surrender, allowing us to relinquish that which no longer serves our highest good. As we *let go* of attachments, expectations, and fears, we liberate ourselves from the shackles of the past and hold the infinite possibilities of the present moment.

o open heart: The practice of opening our hearts is a courageous invitation to vulnerability, authenticity, and connection. By cultivating compassion, forgiveness, and unconditional love, we dissolve the barriers that separate us and expand into the boundless expanse of our true essence.

v visualize: Through the power of visualization, we tap into the creative potential of our soul, envisioning the life we desire with clarity and intention. Visualization becomes a sacred practice of co-creation, aligning our thoughts, emotions, and actions with our deepest aspirations and dreams.

e energize: As energetic beings, we are intimately connected to the vibrational fabric of the universe. By aligning with the frequency of love and abundance, we harmonize with the flow of life, inviting miracles, synchronicities, and blessings into our experience.

. prioritize: Self-love becomes the foundation of our path, guiding us to honor our needs, desires, and boundaries with reverence and compassion. By prioritizing ourselves, we reclaim our inherent worthiness and embody the essence of love in its purest form.

In the grand scope of our existence, we are all called to realize the sacredness of being our full selves. In every breath, every emotion, every pause, and every act of letting go, we embody the essence of love, illuminating the path for ourselves and all beings. As we open our hearts, visualize our dreams, and energetically align with the priority of the highest truth of who we are, we step into the fullness of our potential and radiate love outward, transforming the world one heartbeat at a time.

May this journey be a testament to the infinite power of love, reminding us that in the end, all there is to do is to

***

Acknowledgments

We have something like over sixty thousand thoughts per day. Getting them out of my head and organized into some sort of understanding is the most therapeutic, yet hardest thing I have ever done. And it takes a village.

My beautiful family continues to be a driving force in my life, for which I am eternally grateful. Thank you to my incredible husband and soul partner, David Collins, for your never-ending levels of love and support. You see so much in me and have believed in me since the fateful day we met two and a half decades ago. Your continuous encouragement to be all of me has fueled my walk. It takes a very strong man to be married to this crazy. Your unique and unconditional love makes me the luckiest girl in the world.

You also gifted me with the two most divine children in the world, who have taught me so much about love and life. Brendan and Meghan, I am humbled to learn and grow with you and cherish watching you create your own families. Each new layer opens my heart deeper, and becoming a Nana takes me places I didn't know existed. You inspire me to be the best me I can be, and as our family grows, my desire to do so does as well. Love you all dearly.

Little brother Jeffrey, we have been through so much together. The miles we live apart, combined with the intentionality of our time spent together, is the true embodiment of love. I cherish our priorities and the love of you and your girls. Your home and heart are so warm and inviting, and you continue to fuel me to be the best big sister I can be.

Maid of honor (twice!), you were the first friend I had once I incarnated, and you continue to be my go-to sister. Colleen Marie, your encouragement and support go beyond blood; I am so thankful our mothers had amazing taste in friendship, and we get to continue it.

More space-holding that made this book possible goes beyond family. My avatar for bringing out deep inner knowing lying dormant within is the one and only Scott Kashman. What a perfect blend of psychology guru and comedian. Scott, you bless me with your signature servant leadership style, for which I grow like a weed. This pivotal chapter of life laid the foundation for reflective understanding, and I am eternally grateful.

Soul Sister Sarah, you, too, hold space like no other, fueling this walk, which can definitely feel lonely at times. Thank you for seeing me and for being my fellow disruptor. You gave me the courage to leap, and provided much-needed wind to this ride.

The rise of the female spirit has also been deeply supported by my marketing director, friend, and journey partner, Gail Lamarche. Witnessing your blossoming, Ms. Gail, has been one of the greatest joys of this ride. I also express deep, deep gratitude to my Root Cause

Healing Movement partners, Cara Hewett, Maria Hincapie, and Tracy Zboril. I am forever grateful that the Universe brought us together; the safe and supportive co-creative space you provide brings out the divine best in me.

Last but not least, none of this would have been possible without my friend, editor, co-creator, and publisher, Julie Colvin. When we worked together on *Her Phoenix Rising*, you pushed me to go deeper and unearth parts of my story that I had not yet connected with. You took lots and lots of time to listen and allowed me the opportunity to find my nontraditional voice. And, yes, distilling this offering down to its current, beautiful state took time. You leaned in. Listened some more. Asked lots of excellent questions. Together, we created this unique offering in a way that would not have been possible without you. Julie, please know the freedom and joy you have brought into my life. You help so many of us heal with your safe and inspiring space; please know how much I cherish you.

Notes

---

1   Singer, Michael. *The Untethered Soul: The Journey Beyond Yourself.*
    Oakland: New Harbinger Publications, Inc. 2007.
2   Perry, Bruce, and Oprah Winfrey. *What Happened to You:
    Conversations on Trauma, Resilience, and Healing.* New York:
    Flatiron Books. 2021.
3   Tolle, Eckhart. *A New Earth: Awakening to Your Life's Purpose.*
    New York: Plum/Penguin. 2006.
4   Reklau, Mark. *The Life-Changing Power of Gratitude.*
    Independently published on Amazon. 2018.
5   Nestor, James. *Breath: The New Science of a Lost Art.* New York:
    Riverhead Books/Penguin. 2020.
6   Chopra, Deepak. *Metahuman: Unleashing Your Infinite Potential.*
    New York: Harmony Books/Random House. 2019.
7   Hicks, Esther and Jerry. *The Astonishing Power of Emotions:
    Let Your Feelings Be Your Guide.* New York: 2007.
8   Uhl, Cassie. *The Zenned Out Guide to Understanding Chakras:
    Your Handbook to Understanding the Energy of the Chakra System.*
    New York: Rock Point. 2020.

9   Walsh, Neal Donald. *Conversations with God: Book One.* UK: Hodder & Stoughton. 1997.

10 Holiday, Ryan. *Stillness Is the Key.* New York: Penguin. 2019.

11 Doyle, Glennon. *Untamed.* New York: Random House. 2020.

12 Oxford Reference. *Neuroplasticity Definition.* https://www.oxfordreference.com/display/10.1093/oi/authority.20110803100230276.

13 Andrew Huberman. YouTube. *The Science of Letting Go.* Dec. 22nd, 2021. 4:20, https://www.youtube.com/watch?v=GrYD1b6J6tA.

14 Siegel, Daniel J. *Aware: The Science and Practice of Presence.* New York: A TarcherPerigee Book. 2020.

15 To find out more about HeartMath® Institute's research, resources, and techniques, visit https://www.heartmath.org

16 Doty, James R. *Into the Magic Shop: A Neurosurgeon's Quest to Discover the Mysteries of the Brain and the Secrets of the Heart.* New York: Penguin Random House. 2016.

17 Dispenza, Dr. Joe. *Breaking the Habit of Being Yourself: How to Lose Your Mind and Create a New One.* California: Hay House. 2012.

18 Lipton, Ph.D., Bruce. *The Biology of Belief: Unleashing the Power of Consciousness, Matter & Miracles.* California: Hay House. 2005.

19 Musser, George. *Spooky Action at a Distance: The Phenomenon That Reimagines Space and Time and What It Means for Black Holes, the Big Bang, and Theories of Everything.* New York: Scientific American. 2016.

20 Dispenza, Dr. Joe. *Breaking the Habit of Being Yourself: How to Lose Your Mind and Create a New One.* California: Hay House. 2012

21 Lipton, Ph.D., Bruce. *The Biology of Belief: Unleashing the Power of Consciousness, Matter & Miracles.* California: Hay House. 2005.